Shift Perception

Helen Lopez

Shift Perception

Shearsman Books
Exeter

First published in the United Kingdom in 2009 by
Shearsman Books Ltd
58 Velwell Road
Exeter EX4 4LD

www.shearsman.com

ISBN 978-1-84861-073-6
First edition

Acknowledgements:
Some of these poems were previously published in
Poetry Wales and in *Shearsman*.

Cover image by Helen Lopez

CONTENTS

To Chris

TEMPER RELIEF

This resting home is for yesterday's sex workers
where the wild cat strikes and the capital gains
air. In this region of challenged sentences there
is the largest loss of temper relief. With Virgin
money can you buy patriotic rhetoric and a
competition that will mop up the absurdity
(of life) in a cultural shift? Change that
respects women to the highest degree
involves glamour model celebrations of old
sexism. This will assess my breast and generate

marks out of ten-type entertainment in their
language of choice. The military concurs with
 democratic process while participating in
a cultural chasm. How well we can make judgments
from the fireside coffee table. If he is a rational
president delivering the right message, he deserves a
pat on the back and a huge prize that will distract
attention from kick-backing influence. This will
signal the right path and gently wean leaders
away from corruption that ultimately

vomits on the shoes of aid donators. The key
word approach in box classification connection
is a view of the world which organises knowledge for
all. Then when and if the new look cross-border
attacks, linked to disease and that poison relations, have
now changed course to a war on obesity. There is some
active support for unplanned headlong qualifications of
choice making the prime factor almost always and
without exception, a divisive memory. If you have a
body mass index of 29 you are very nearly obese.

Associated Diseases

A peer reviewed thesis has produced a
healthcare political time bomb. Long

before the advent of the straight
forward answer was the yardstick spike.

Goal posts were moved overnight
regularly declaring a new reality

that was conclusive and beyond debate.
The correlation between evidence and the

emphasis uptake declares that voters were
treated as an afterthought on this already

congested island where phrasemongers
war with misleading statistics and

sloganisation. They go into the water with
their bomb-making training material, and

people systems crush the rebels with
research evidence that tows the line.

DEAD DOGS

The problem with big space projects is that
there are fewer national caveats failing
to meet objectives. Stripped of
responsibilities, chess board killers offer
dead dogs drinks for want of temperate
language. The risk to the public is quite
small if one claps at the end of a video
conference. 14 poppy free provinces but
NATO could do better. *The soul makes
guns go off*—a tick box for isolating the
extremist. In the garden after lunch
where the bougainvillea rains, I shall water
the saladini both fresh and weary.
If you lower your voice you can defeat
her screams as another rebel group
withdraws. The unhappy Secretary
General is staying the course 'no fast exit'
shielded again by temperate language.

9.11.07

The potential vagueness of language is in
the mouth of social space. Big theatre
discourse on terrorism amounts to living
with fireworks spent on the beach; thunder
clap/canon and lethal tank. The *longslow*
sweep away of our moral refuse failed to
bring about change and China sets its sight
on the moon. You row your own boat and
I will swim as language, and move on—
like water. "What a fiasco"—Lowering the
upper limit of compensation help to
rebuild your life and home. With a decade
long free kick family friendly borrowing
policy there has been an appalling
catalogue of serious error in judgement.
We might as well have turned to the
barmaid who can crush beer cans in her
bare breasts and hang spoons from her
nipples to bring in the customers.

Avoid the Art Market

The reclaimed oak hedgehog house
arrived eventually as the postal workers

returned to work. Our best top tip for
radicalising and indoctrinating a

welcoming committee of school children
is the next step forward on the mission

in pursuit of truth and short term tricks.
They say they don't target civilians and

suicide bombers can opt out in the south.
The sea (her inspiration) had been exciting

that morning. She said "I haven't been
out of my way for these pictures".

COUPONS

Is he all spin and no substance?
(Who Cares) Legally binding omission
limits would be expected in eco towns
occupied by *catslikefelix* with rising
aspirations and challenges for the future.
Top down centralising pancakes of draft
legislations that will harmonise the
judiciary and the executive power sharing
arrangement deal—when waterfalls came
to her in a dream, like a delayed dusting of
snow on the hills remembered when
slamming tennis balls across an open
space. The mouth space opens and shuts
for language a landscape.

DYNASTY

It is time for sacrifices; ban bullying at
work now, as the time has come to
measure out the world in wonderful
restaurants. The mass protest march went
off like a mammoth conic fountain in a
counter coup – grandiose and in earnest.
She is subtle in her criticism while
focusing on how best to mobilise a
protest on the street during a spell of house
arrest. A change of tone was noted as the
hair shirts came off the so utterly
recognisable silent clowns seen towing the
party line. Good old dramas where the id
is let loose in the body.

PERMIT

Tensions are
palpable and
the law has
made fools
of us all
putting public
safety at risk.
What went
wrong? He
texted a friend
and London
on a heightened
state of alert
let shooting
an innocent
become a
breach of
health and
safety.
Commander
control lost
the strapline
and had no
idea the
radios didn't
work underground.
Major failings,
serious and
avoidable errors
meant the
implementation of
order to stop
was preceded by
shoot on sight.

Fabric Wrap

Less money all round for good causes
and the must have toys under the

tree this Christmas of which 80% will
come from China (in the space race)

this year. Half a mile away 'element b' a
bomb disabling device sat waiting out a

glitch in the supply chain system that
had failed to flag up its availability.

HARVEST

As the fear of floods diminished,
gathered and pressed leaves are scattered.
We succumb to force feeding because
shapely women give birth to more
intelligent babies. A teenage killer posted
several messages about his interests in
guns on unspace before his rampage. A
voluntary recall perusing the state of
emergency on the hotplate of a pistachio
Aga drips on reclaimed teak flooring from
Preservation in Action. There is a national
shortage of normal control brains. Only
just outside on the decked veranda which
extends the family room into the garden
there is a difficult call to make. Watchful
for commitment signals—complaints are
addressed as there is a statutory right to
raise concerns about work surfaces that
don't come up to scratch.

Students — The Vanguard of Protest

Stave off bad news day found the surge
was not as high as expected at the geek
girl diner where the economy remains
robust and costs get passed on. The
nationalist grip quashed the ministry of
information and there was chaos on
campus. The nice western policies and the
price of oil flies the flag of big is best
when it is quite obvious that less is more at
the end of the day. Would that be the view
across the high street? A downturn
working at the heart of our company and
keeping the pound strong is nothing more
than a forest in crisis. Deeply technical
women as role models can defend your
fragile democracy with physical and legal
attacks with a gooey/gooee and a gooi. A
goowy in a nutshell or in the hand will
manage that digital lifestyle we have
come to know and love/hate, you choose.

BOXING IN THE PIPES

"Lot 555 white ceramic vases—no,
in the skip they go." The advantages of
having a project manager who buys one
and gets one free is that they are much
more in keeping with condiments close at
hand. "An oriental blue and white charger
10, 5—anyone? 2, 2 I'm bid, 4, 4 bid . . ."
Ideas to steal for an organised larder in
New England style tradition—dream
kitchen. ". . . 6 bid, 6 should be double that,
lovely for the Christmas table . . ." He
always thought painted units were a good
idea until gutting and remodelling went
out of fashion. ". . . 6 sold and away, 114,
quality lot that. Zenith 35mm Camera Lot
561, 2 on the camera, 2 pound on him,
sold and away at 2 pound, err I'll take 3, 5,
7 I'm bid, all out sir, ladies bid on my
right, 9, 9 and off." In the new extension
there is room for an extra table and tree at
Christmas and even in winter it feels like
summer.

THE ROT SET IN

Immense pinnacles of equity release, asset
rich and cash poor an international harvest
festival. Consider this special relationship;
mandarins who make policy will stand up
and endure this ruthless adversity—obesity
is every body's business and the big issue
is reflected in a local survey. Flexible
working arrangements will make time
eventually. A body mass protest. An
essential conduit such as this necessitates

scrutiny far and above the cover up of
getting on and doing something, anything.
It is best to accept advice on a serious
issue, establish the full nature and scale of
the domain, where gaps are located
evidence must be found. Abandon spin
and embrace denied allegations for old
time's sake. Please don't give me all the
facts unless I ask. A prayer for ancillary
relief before lunch helps the day along

nicely, until an outbreak of particularly
dirty attacks is pedalled by ministers on
the *treats from the trolley* at teatime. Our
experts work terribly hard. They are very
well placed to help evoke terror in the
small private producers. The cost of
alcohol is killed to order as we ask—
where is the Christmas turkey now? Vets
on the ground found strains in the
meanings of classical music. A dirty bomb

would not solve the problem of birds mingling, on this scale it would amount to underkill. And anyway people will have to put something on the table this Christmas. Eternally new carbon copy can always wither and die with the proper exposure. We are going backwards and the inmates fear going home for a happy lifestyle in an alcohol free house. Out of hours the nine o'clock watershed subsides and the national

audit office celebrates a clean bill of health.
and is found hiding intoxicated. An addiction
that affects the whole family. The full story is
a shadow. Suffering from depression now is
a bad sign just before the analysis of the issue is
complete. Forecasters can never rely on
the weather. The budget airline backed
modest increases retrospectively
and the reality of this strain spelt a new
interest in reparation for all.

FASHIONABLE TURKEYS

Christmas best/worst time of year (when
the cost of living goes up) and luxury is

not what it used to be. Rational
individualism blinds the fashionable elite

and we were robbed this morning of the
sharp frost. Into the woods the

independent wage earners cruise with
readiness to kill themselves on behalf of

their community. Luxury is diminished by
a mass fashion suicide in front of the new

god, the poor and oppressed survived, just.
Ubiquitous handbags are worn the wrong

way by lower middleclass terrorists
busying themselves with a double

standard. Take art—it is always confusing to
the burgeoning buying class—an especially

sequestered identity. *Vintage* bamboozles
them and preys on the primary rule of

fashion—group ethos that rigs the show
with predetermined results.

MEETING OF MINDS

Have the government of all the talents
found a partially identified fail safe
measure? This choice of words is a little
disingenuous. A substantial period of time
may help confirm in some people's minds
a deep forensic search, a spindle with
some security and more hand luggage.

Pave the way and track the minister's
pronouncements; the vehicle exclusion
zones and our man in Pakistan are on the
agenda. A complete gift remains found
and is designed out of the building to cut
the much needed ice with a rhesus
monkey. A whirlwind that tests our u-turn

nerve. The squeeze on credit is a resulting
symptom of wider moral collapse. The
navigator ejected the two point agenda
with a slow and intermittent internet
connection. Steer a course past the
privileged utility worker who wants to be
luckier than anyone else. The big breasts

of Fleet Street (crystal clear of student
debt) want to see Westminster move the
couch and the cat in push meetings. A
larger than life fog lingers and fails to
meet the aspirations of the people. Deal or
no deal on the route to growth and a
bright future's investment net goal/gain.

LIFE IS A BEACH

What about the mechanisms of
parliamentary arithmetic, when rubber
stamps a spot of gunshot residue beyond
which a crucial philosophical argument
sets out to salami slice our identity. When
considered objectively and at an early
stage the merits of this issue seem light
enough to just add water to the Magna
Carta. The normal law of the land slides
into a state of emergency. This set of
criteria speaks with one voice about
firearms and their discharge of muddled
thinking. He is in pursuit of a trivial
dispute and hustling a front bench job.

The house gave up another of its secrets. The amount of cod caught in British waters was increased during the time it took to dig up the garden. A negotiated settlement found a second body in the *art lost register*. The loft survey forum prefers to clad with 10 inches of fleece, for joyous free time with a foreign wife. The Queen focused on her destiny and took up pole dancing, this lack of planning filtered out to the art market. What is the point of the moon? An interesting place to do science, exploration/exploitation, and soon a conventional space travel destination.

RAPID EXPANSION

Obesity is equal to climate change; an
ongoing debate. Space tourism

at package holiday prices of the
Goldilocks planets—not too hot, not too

cold. Sentient lifers eat porridge on regular
traffic to Mars with remote stopovers that

study their weight gain/loss. We are not
by any means alone at the drop in

prayer and retreat centre. With the passage
of time and a decent audit trail, behold

there will be a sound to reflect on.
The number of pipes to be insulated will

depend on making cricket sexy for the
so called rescuers of the son of God.

NEW MONEY

In this misery memoir he dumped his
desire in west London a goldmine in the
wrong hands. Beneficial joint tenants
online or tenants in common offline.
Wearing leaf green and magenta she set
off alarm bells. Non encrypted missing
disks of double doors—a time based
artwork in paper print and paste. A limited
budget amount of background digging
brought to light the gravity of what ground
rules had been broken. Blue sky e-crime
thin slices the increasingly pessimistic
reclassification of data protection without
law, in the right/wrong hands, that is
everyone with kids. Noticeably there will
be a small rise in the share price and a
downturn of good information for would
be buy to let property developers who
snake and ladder across the board.

A TIME TO SHINE

1. Rise Above

Start up by nurturing success, aim high
steal ideas, net work. This is *real time*
research by the experts roaming the room
in a culture of enterprise and a living
system with flexible funding solutions.
This is a time to shine the net effects on
the stock of geographic indicators,
dynamic and innovative processes in place
with a clear mandate for leadership. This
snapshot will inform policy and decide the
churn rate of team breakdown. This paints
a vision for the future on an economic
development canvas, stretched and ready
to boomerang straight back the trends in
the right direction. It is service to say that
with our foot on the gas our geography is
an asset. 3 hubs in our engine room
manage and lead space, skills and strands.
Fleet of foot and with a single slide we
operate in a vacuum of heavy
manufacturing.

2. Uncommon Results

The gross added value sustaining the
community in physical spaces has
processes in place for project failure that
shape the retail and leisure hub. A footfall
comes in as a positive lever in the public
sector, and in the right time frame we
could have a symbiotic relationship. The
trick there and here, in a winter
wonderland is to maximise the benefits of
eco prioritisation in a global Christmas
market. Clever knowledge industries
manage and lead the spirit of partnership
with the right solutions going forward.
Light composite materials spend alone and
give up sovereignty for the greater good.
Clever stuff—creative industries, a prize
winning local supplier, distinctive and
unique along the costal strip we have the
sea. The time is right for small and
medium sized leisure opportunities,
businesses that will endure and shine.

3. What's In It for Me?

When you set out goals and activities for
the year break into your creativity.
Brainstorm your thought shower. "You are
always only 12ft from an opportunity."
Look back on your life with 20/20 vision,
manage your memories and then lay them
to rest. Mainstream the diversity
contractor with key icons, opportunities
come hidden, camouflaged and sometimes
on a plate. Seize and be aware of the
abundance theory in hindsight develop
your sagacity, try more little and often and
discover the habit of flipping the negative.
Only visit with pit stop pessimisms.
Bounce back fuelled by meaning. Go the
extra yard and mexican wave your future
by living and breathing the bigger picture.
Define your elephant thick skin with your
yes/no quota and connect with others.
Multiplicity in action and disruptive
thinking make good quality conversation
when you need to get going.

4. In Good Stead

Be the best you already are—your future your choice. The science of rapport has a formula for success. There you go, wherever you are. Even at a visioning meeting navigate your dreams with a search engine for charisma. This is root canal surgery for fear and don't forget to bring passion to work with you. You will get what you always get if you do what you always do. Discount the future cash streams with highly desirable phases of travel. The absolute grail is a big step forward that clarifies the concept and hugs people. Focus above the hurdles, seek approval and the project will champion clout. Smart goals have beautiful outcomes. The mission statement has specific hidden agendas that lifestyle your leadership gurus with a contingency plan.

5. Breakout Session

How do you know what you have got at
the end of the day? A novel set of
interrelated activities that trade off each
other until their end performance. Tot
them up for the bottom line and
domesticate the logic because this is a
complicated network of dependency.
For what it is worth phase and lay against
the calendar the point of no return where
ideas ought to be chasing the money.
Expand the lift efficiency of current
capacity, monitoring and controlling
the completion handover sign off. A
logical sequence of tracked events and
operations are ultimately closed down.

CHANNEL HOPPING IN THE AFTERNOON

So he came around threatening me in
Brazil – Christ the redeemer was built so
she could feel better and get the sleep she
needed. Plug into service and price; make
your Christmas dream come true. Ladies
and gentlemen hiya, you don't believe he
is the father do you? You, safe behind a
woman's skirts yuba duba doo. The
deadline—22nd December by 2pm for
Christmas delivery looking so good is a
doggone shame and your repayments
won't change. *How clean is your house?* is
sponsored by Kleeneze. Do you have his
labs back yet. He is fine let him go. We go
sublime lovers entwine make love your
goal in cities. Liverpool has been the
world's biggest revolving door, sucking
people in and spitting people out. Give me
a chance and I will prove this, aren't they
amazing walking the dog across a wet
field it sounds funny I know but I feel safe
in them. Borderline crumpet, not a trendy
trendy trendy bird forget our price, right
now I will have a cup of tea please, this is
the place to be with me.

I'm having a massage party tonight—go on
come I am inviting you. Why don't we go
out and grab a movie or something, she is
doing it again where does her anger come
from. Hello yes speaking who is that,
never mind who I am it's a moonshine war
and the federal authorities are here all
ready. And you invited them because you
are involved in young people's lives and a
miracle happened and the Menorah
continued to burn for 8 days. Yes my
name is Ickle Piggle Woo and I climbed a
tree and this is bad and much more prone
to bleeding when I was at the TUC this
year. News and sport in 15 minutes and
every 15 minutes Boss fragrances for men
with 152 to put Sri Lanka in a strong
position. It is a massive disappointment—
the watchdog's annual report says target,
because he thinks it is a good story. Angry
bees spotted by the Pakistani umpire at the
hub of supporting centres (a late headline)
and Thomas and his friends are busy
delivering the mail—go to sleep Upsy
Daisy, hey guys look what's on T.V.

If I aint got you I aint got nothing to do
battle with to qualify for the world's
strongest man who hasn't even got a
husband. Breathless I think I am going to
have to pass, the bigger the challenge the
more you need Duracell and we will send
it straight to your daughter. So
comfortable to move in and for sitting on
the sofa and in the last two days I have
seen them wearing them, so go on try
something new today. A little bit to go yet,
it's like breaking a skin on a rice pudding
or something. This year to save me from
tears I'll give it to someone special. You
need to go back on insulin, and you are
probably right what name should we use
today for those that came into the area and
are missing in the story behind the sound
bites. The next visit I will do better I will
work harder, junk—I beg your pardon.
You went off the rails didn't you; around
the corner here aim to give the children the
best possible start.

MATTER OUT OF PLACE

An overwhelming tsunami of emotion in
the magic garden where Bougainvillea
flowers rain on you, has a relationship
with Monet's *serious* paintings and better
still Matisse's late paper cut-outs. An
entirely legitimate deconstruction of
reality that gains momentum as the
audience are let off the leash, at last, in a
one-a-day way. The interrogation of
language in sub prime peripheral factors
makes good copy of a ridiculous and
appalling situation. A more Christmassy
Christmas for whistle blowers, spies,

sharks and spivs when the fallout from a
government blunder bequeaths a slush
fund of a hundred leading stars. A kiss, a
smile and taste the difference vintage cava
that speculates on etiquette, the best way
to categorize people. Retail physiologists
log too many callers that stack up ahead of
the fraudster terribly nervous about things
that haven't gone wrong. Random number
generation is fool proof. In an epidemic of
reading failure a teddy bear named
Mohammed holds talks with a spent force in
the nation states. The Federal Reserve

slowdown is the confluence of all these factors. The Chinese aren't ready to talk trade—remember they are busy with the space race. Family fortunes can change in Euro zone with a gift card for pro-hunting campaigners and in the great hall of the people they cathect the space shuttle and block the EU trade gap with widening money men. The backlash of third party donations is your hair's worst nightmare. There were whispers of "we are very worried" which expanded into a crisis for the general in his second skin.

OPEN PROBLEM

The golden section package for bright
young things, who know sleaze when they
see it, has a clear glance at beautiful
properties. The letter of the law could have
dished out 40 lashes in infinite recursive
sequence. Ominously, barriers are erected
with crushed amoretti biscuits, between
the moral majority and fundamental
platitudes. Watching this unfold (as we do)
and preferring bigger deceptions for nobler
causes, it is obvious there are serious
issues with the funding arrangements and
credit isn't what it used to be, all mystery
and magic.

Remain sceptical

The sum total of every choice you have ever made is a multiplicity of action in thinking in or outside the basket. A case in hand with personal space is the *Cultural Change Initiative*- for individuals who are serious about their leadership. Select the coarse design alternatives and refine getting into detail. Imagine it—cash surplus, growth and sustainability. Money is incurred. Do you know when to fear loud noises and falling over? And—are your dreams big enough? Or is it all risk and uncertainty with the birds? Hot water is a frequent presence on the airwaves. This old lag in a difficult period comes to the fore for a moment of truth. Indicative of the kinds of smoke coming out of her ears and in the heart of present circumstances she found the courage for the long haul. Outcome and pole standing, an escalation out of all proportion with rigorous intellectual argument stirring up strong feelings. The incredible mega statue got a grip on events and we see a totally disproportionate punishment from this point of view. It would have to take a parliamentary contest to surmise early the really encouraging bottom of this question. Enduring doubts grow from strength to strength hidden in the tragic details of the

laws of the land. Raked over
and forbidding various kinds of speech
freedoms e-mail any dot and ask for
closure. Controversial speakers spark and
bowl media googlies and the newspapers
will sell the principles in this case. As the
affair with Teddy comes to an end, the
prisoner declares she "bears no grudge".
The political imperative here is how this
deal was brokered and with whose
sensitivity in mind. A broad point fully
disguising doubts again and how agonising
it is to watch the fallout. She came to
terms somehow with *absolute* freedom.
The policy unit will enter talks on the

issue of affiliation with traders serving your area. This one off, useful and slightly more opaque emergency number is parcelling up the money in self-interest. The transparent system bit them hard in opposition and the basis for going forward will need goodwill on both sides. The key issue in this political levy for the long term is through the back door and around the table. A Punch and Judy change of heart presents a vexed question and uses trawling for money as a way forward, because you don't want to be caught short when Christmas is coming. The question is—should we give goats and ploughs just

after three or wait till supper time when
clearly there will be an enquiry.

Proxy donations ascertain all matters
concerning hammering out a settlement
that may move to be a greater role in
negotiating a night out and maybe a show
on the town. A long time supporter
assumed that it would be legal and
understood that to make changes would
cost money. And from her snow cave the
achingly hip green officer collects data for
Ben and Jerry's Climate Change College.
In his five years of disappearance the
canoeist could have known Chunky

Monkey and loved Cherry Garcia as we
do. Who knows? Global warming is the
new black in this leadership campaign.
At the centre for galvanised explosive use
of fossil fuels everything is driven by
business as *a good neighbour.* Ethics are
all the rage—profitable, and barking up
the wrong tree. It is just a problem not a
disaster, 'it will be fine like.' A woman on
the edge and in the eye of a media storm;
and all in the run up to Christmas too as
Tesco calls for a cut in interest rates. Do
retailers drown their cries of woe with
Prosecco?

BEARER BOUND

She banked her head in a paintless mess,
a real fear that deals in nutshells on a

standard night. Light walks through,
timeless, and it is now what she

thought it was. The truth is cyclical
weakness and high confidence at the

same time. We wake up and today it is not
the case, it can't happen and left alone

we fall in, slowing or pushed we stretch
a fraction, talk and fret a bit.

Dual Use

The red western died in a swimming pool with stars at a fashionable hotel and the pragmatic ambassador assured them his gift was legal and declared on 400 and 2 for 8 weapons of mass destruction, a healthy weight of growth. This nuclear confession of current intentions quickly converted the overt program exclusively to move/correct their views into back down. In respect of the dossier and hands tied by inflation they still have a belief within themselves and remain 100% focused on operating a huge fleet of stretch limousines. A US intelligent assessment of media interest had the banks chasing money, balancing risk with weaponisation because of history and the global squeeze on clean air credit.

SHIFT PERCEPTION

Lashed to the mast of another's ship watch
this train crash and air brush out
inconvenient truths, when each rehearsed
mouthful of sound becomes more prime

ministerial each week in the ethical
workshop called in to do running repairs in
human sympathy—'You can say that
again.' Abjectly devastated he shot your

fox; a glittering career is an assumption
and not in the round. An attractive future
out of failure rises from the ashes or
perhaps just rearranges itself closer to the

data. He took off his spectacles and
wondered what had tipped the balance in
favour of switching faith by the existing
workforce who voted with their feet.

Mass ASBO

A committed but
unlikely terrorist
with real world
interests made a
desirable turn and
puts a floor under
the slowdown and
the lumber Jills
and land girls
believe a quarter
percent is definitely
better than nothing
in this iconic
scenery where
raging house
prices are a thing
of the past and
cowards carry out
odious acts
for the part
time jester
secretary knowing
full and well
that smaller
prisons perform
better and that
the harder you
try the better you
get at the
trickier aspects of
human experience.

NORMAL PRECAUTIONS

It takes time for a law to mature its thin angry
blue line, breed and knit together a rural life upon a single
photon. Sources for the poems of the lyrical

terrorist are set with some frequency and collusion.
This lunchtime when great music speaks to the people
and on the face of it a world class education steps into

the limelight with girlish relish. We see she takes her pop
seriously. For the protectorate war might be the
legal option and the status quo though miserable and

undesirable, chimes with the instincts of the party. A strange
tongue marks the nature of this relationship de facto and
boxing is the *social glue* on the ground.

SHOULD WE EAT CHERRIES IN WINTER?

Bears trap loose and weak coalitions,
they bristle them with activity and then
ratchet up a gear by sprouting dangerous
levels of rhetoric. This is savvy politics
with paralysed focus sending its people
fleeing to the refuge of churches and
airports. Bears that whip up and fudge a
Ukrainian style uprising. A scream speech
full and frank from the operations director
—a defining moment—he admits a gigantic
failure of project planning and tentatively
hopes he can dig himself out of the snow.

LYRICAL SCRAP

In the garden after lunch where the
bougainvillea rains, I shall water

the saladini both fresh and weary.
You row your own boat and I will swim as

language, and move on—like water.
When waterfalls came in a dream,

like a delayed dusting of snow on the hills
remembered when slamming tennis balls

across an open space. The mouth space
opens and shuts for language a landscape.

Free wi-fi @ McDonalds

Background overview
to take forward how
best to conduit a career
break business support
dynamo fully aware
recruitment enterprise
education thematic
reports people in power
to supplement your
key outputs massive
case studies overall

document normalising
entrepreneurship
can do attitude
IMS training is
everything post
training mentoring
presentation skills
course focused on story
telling develop the
package bolt on world
of work enterprise

workshop with Jordan
glamour model
entrepreneur a leap
significant shift
effective job groups
work place learning
choices free wi-fi@
McDonalds a central
plank interview game
with career ideas zippy
wizzy resources tools

e-progress files break the
mould be your own
boss ideas factory
broadening horizons
support team action
planning learning skills
presentation documents
achievement evidence
reflect and take action
decision making
organisation.

MECHANISM

Monarchs use the sun as a compass to guide them on their 2000 mile round trip booking a holiday is a great way of beating the post-Christmas blues the key gene CRY2 identified in the monarch butterfly that acts as a biological clock for estimating the 24-hour cycle of the circadian rhythm because Britons (even in a credit squeeze) are far more likely to cut down on the big ticket items and luxury consumer goods than on their beloved holidays cryptochrome—a light sensitive protein which counts the passing hours of each day and also communicates the information to the monarch's inbuilt solar compass for the insect to calculate its correct direction of flight the appallingly wet summer last year will encourage more of us to head abroad and swap the UK's unpredictable climate for guaranteed sunshine we have still to understand how the tiny brain of the Monarch butterfly which is no bigger than the head of a ball point pen can arrange information about time and space that leads it to carry out the appropriate flight behaviour.

STORM

And then there was splash and boom and I had to collect up
what I heard and what I saw into a box a text box for use later
and I had to go back and collect not back but just scroll a bit
and find the box to put the splash and the boom in and my arm
was caught around something warm and good but I had to
turn not wanting to take my arm and move and lose the warm
and the good so I kept missing the box the text box which was
white and empty and should have the boom and the splash in it
for later for the collection

hel*love*nice

We turn reluctantly

from the water only to cross it again

Venezia, filter tips and confetti

rose carmine ochre and hookers green

Did she look in the rear view mirror

before meeting the Prophet

(peace be upon him)-

can that be said?

The peacocks will

make themselves heard

THE GRITTERS WERE OUT

On a star lit evening an articulated wagon awaits as we find
out that this haulier doesn't insure Art in transit to Kensington
Gore or anywhere, we pay the money and send it anyway.
Someone lives on a house boat and has a gorgeous kitten with
yellow eyes. Plate Tectonics is at the bottom of all this, it fuels
our planet and our seasons make time for knitting. A cigarette
left burning on a shelf, while he tends to a customer; there are
black scald marks where others have been left smouldering
before. Don't you just hate the words bespoke and mezzanine
or is it just me that prefers elbow and voluptuous. I make a fire
for company more than warmth it really doesn't throw any
heat but it crackles and looks appealing. At the buffet dinner
she adeptly tackled her drumstick with a plastic knife and fork
and everything she had selected stayed on the plate.

WINWITHVISA

everything is premier and

language leaks all over the place in this panic plan

a prism through which we see everything is the fiscal stimulus
        package of

compulsory intervention by Somali pirates who know from
        experience

that it helps to have pointed wings when flying by your wits alone

into an unprecedented package of parasitic measures

the radiance is reflected and what a feeling that is and then

looking forward

to a cooling big night of dual relief

In the woods

at Englishman river falls
the bears are earning good money
for grilling

from the scat on the ground it looked like
they had been eating blueberries

we're here for the long haul
ole opal eyes – rising to the occasion
with stops on request

As Winter Sets In

As winter sets in the holistic shared ownership and couch
surfing redwing tribes fly in from Iceland, they travel with
hope through a media storm in a teacup. We will pay homage
to Dave from Aviva who will manage our expectations for
the repairs to the roof from storm damage. Dark space, does
it matter? A three star authority lives with hope (not good
enough) disquiet guidance is a tricky transition. All fixed
cameras are painted yellow and the coyote community is in
a transit camp for the 4th quarter of infrastructure spending.
Manage the stock mop up the surplus flow over short term
impact. Stave off China chipping in, point the way to a better
deal and a social safety net.

DROP LOCK

Our tracker reaches drop lock and switches time to the fixed option and now
in failing modified night flights of the not to distant future
with time to think (a recreational pursuit)
about regeneration projects
and a lie to oneself
that involves
distance
hopes / dreams
the fleeting nature of history and we remember only just
in time that it is the fool who moves mountains with expression
and a new awareness drawing in free-model and by the way all my toys are in pink now.

Entrepreneur Exchange

Save Money
Make Money
Ask me now!
driven by European
media convergence
which can
take everything
forward
to the cusp
of change
we are in
a position
to redeploy / relocate
it's a good hook
to hang
a close-knit
second term
overchieved
by champions

LOTTO

The performance based
funding formula will
prove its value
with a podium finish.

Gap to Podium
a simple equation
at the cost of less Art
and good causes.

Boxing (the social
glue on the ground)
is the / our best bet for a
podium finish.

SYLVIA

Free run chicken and greens
barefoot Dungeness half crab

going fishing destinations
with breading and batter mixes

born to fish and running a grab
called Captain America

Gulp is great it is biodegradable
shore lunch window fashion

THINK FAST

Sweet young things working in the Guggenheims acknowledge time, inspire and fire us up. The banks ebb crippled by indecision and remanded in custody with the wrong dietary advice. What is the chance? The traction working our lives leverage/ debt voodoo/ignorance little models speculating on what the territory will look like. Time spent planning with a map for when you walk through hell you must walk faster and big bang day sees watchers in the workplace lining up for weigh-ins. I'm all for visceral risk and adverse trade in tulips I just love to sit back and watch it all fall apart don't you?

www.ingramcontent.com/pod-product-compliance
Lightning Source LLC
Chambersburg PA
CBHW031932080426
42734CB00007B/645